Property Perfection

Asset Protection, Seasonal Savvy, and Aesthetic Excellence

Elaine M. Simpson
Founder & President
Occupancy Solutions LLC

For information address Goodrich Publishing, 2666 CR 247, Moulton, TX 77975

This book may be purchased for educational, business, or promotional purposes. For information, please email esimpson@occupancysolutions.com

Published by Goodrich Publishing
Moulton, TX
GoodrichPublishing.com

ISBN-13: 978-1-7339963-5-8

TABLE OF CONTENTS

INTRODUCTION

The highs and lows of property management are not for the faint of heart. Any of us in the business knows that each day brings challenges, sometimes in the form of obstacles and sometimes in the form of abundant success. The end of each lease, month, year, or decade shares a story of the past, and if we are tuned into the past, we can correct past mistakes. When we learn our lessons, we can somewhat predict future outcomes. More importantly, when we are engaged in the current trends and needs of the present society, we can pivot to meet the needs of our current and future residents.

Recent research discovered that a customer is four times more likely to buy from a competitor if the problem is service related rather than price or product related. Additionally, it takes 12 positive customer experiences to make up for one negative experience, and more than half of all customers share their bad experiences with others.

More than at any other time in property management history, the customer experience is the most important aspect for prospective and current residents. People of all ages demand more for their investment, raise the bar of expectations and speak up about the treatment they deserve. As property managers, we always have our work cut out for us, and it is no surprise that shifting to this new direction has its challenges. However, when we rise to meet our challenges, we beat our competition and, therefore, sign more new residents and retain existing residents.

Welcome to "Property Perfection: Asset Protection, Seasonal Savvy, & Aesthetic Excellence," the latest comprehensive compact handbook by Elaine Simpson, a leading expert in property management. This essential guide is tailored specifically for property owners, managers, and employees of multifamily properties in the United States. It is the first in this captivating series of three mini reference books.

In today's competitive real estate market, maintaining and enhancing the value of your communities is crucial. This compact handbook provides knowledge and practical advice to ensure your properties retain value and stand out.

"Property Perfection" delves into three core aspects of property management: asset protection, seasonal savvy, and aesthetic excellence. Each chapter is packed with tips, best practices, and real-life examples that will empower you to make informed decisions and maximize the potential of your properties.

Asset protection is the foundation of any successful property management strategy. Learn how to safeguard your investment with robust insurance policies, maintenance schedules, and risk management techniques. Our seasonal savvy section will guide you through the unique challenges that each season brings, offering valuable insights on how to prepare your properties for changing weather conditions and market trends. Finally, aesthetic excellence is the cherry on top that will attract and retain residents, ensuring your properties remain in high demand.

This compact handbook is designed to be concise and accessible, allowing you to quickly reference the information you need as you face the day-to-day challenges of property management. Each section is accompanied by checklists, templates, and resources that will simplify your workflow and enhance efficiency.

Join Elaine Simpson as she shares her wealth of experience and knowledge in "Property Perfection: Asset Protection, Seasonal Savvy, & Aesthetic Excellence." With over 35 years in this business, countless lease-ups, thousands of advice blogs, hundreds of speaking engagements, and training countless property management professionals, Elaine knows success comes in one of three ways: hard work, focus on a stellar customer experience, and sometimes a little luck. With this compact handbook, you'll be well-equipped to achieve property management success and set your properties apart in a crowded market.

SECTION 1: ASSET PROTECTION

1: THE POWER OF THE POSITIVE "NO."

How many times a day do you say "no" to a resident or prospect? My guess is a lot! Our communities have many policies, regulations, and requirements that we must enforce as part of our job. Remember, nobody likes getting rejected, and when you say no, it can feel to your customer like a rejection. If someone asks a question to which you must reply "no," try affirming it or offering an alternative. Often, this is a very subtle difference that can make a positive impression. Below are some examples of this process:

- Instead of stating, "Your income does not meet our requirement." try saying, "Your income is below our income requirement."

- Instead of stating, "No, we don't have three-bedroom apartments." try saying, "We have extra-large one- and two-bedroom apartments."

- Instead of stating, "We don't accept pets." try stating, "We are a pet-free community."

- Instead of stating, "You cannot park in that area." try saying, "For your convenience, we offer parking to the right of your building."

To provide exceptional customer service while enforcing rules, practicing the power of the positive "no" as a team is best. Below are some steps to brainstorm with your team to master this technique:

1. Recognize the differences between negative, positive, and neutral phrases in customer/resident situations.

2. List and analyze the standard service phrases your team currently uses.

3. Identify what makes the statement harmful and what not to say in these situations.

4. Apply a list of customer-friendly phrases using the power of the positive "no" for their daily resident/prospect interactions, including challenging situations for your community listed in #2.

5. Role-play and practice using the positive "no."

Sometimes, saying "no" is your only option, especially when correcting resident behavior or enforcing health and safety rules. But, if you practice using the positive "no" in most interactions, when you have to say "no," the impact is much more substantial, and the message is clearer to the person hearing it.

2: Creating Welcome Paperwork

Paperwork can be challenging to put together for the new residents leasing your apartments. Providing the best customer experience, building loyalty, retaining residents, and making sure you consistently receive good reviews can all be affected by the initial paperwork. Of course, certain rules, regulations, and policies need to be conveyed, but you also want them to feel comfortable while moving into their new home.

When future residents feel welcome, they feel important and know how much they mean to you. Integrating a new resident into their living space extends beyond a simple lease signing—it's a profound opportunity to make them feel truly at home. As part of this process, numerous options exist for familiarizing the residents with their new environment.

For instance, consider conducting an in-depth tour of their new home, ensuring they understand its distinctive features and advantages. During this walkthrough, you could point out essential items such as the circuit breaker box and the reset button for the garbage disposal, thus empowering them with knowledge of their residence's functionalities.

You can further enhance their settling-in experience by demonstrating the amenities available. This would entail showing them where these amenities are located and detailing their operating hours and usage guidelines.

You could also offer personalized advice or recommendations based on their lifestyle or preferences. This could range from nearby points of interest, such as parks or restaurants, to insider tips about living in the neighborhood. This is an excellent chance to add a personal touch, making the resident feel cared for and welcome.

Every interaction during this phase allows the new resident to feel at home, valued, and fully equipped for their new living environment. Your approach can shape their first impressions significantly, leading to a comfortable, happy residency. Therefore, it's essential to make a substantial positive impact during the "ultimate demonstration experience."

You should constantly monitor and review how welcome you make your residents feel. Efforts to make our residents feel welcome are not a single action or resolution. It requires multiple efforts over time with planned continuous work in progress.

Developing a comprehensive lease and community rules and regulations for your residents can be challenging. Ensuring you cover everything so that you and your residents are fully protected requires a high level of expertise. Here are some ideas to get you started on executing your Demonstration Plan.

Be Welcoming! The first thing your new resident needs to see from you is that you and your staff are happy to have them be reassured that choosing your community was the right decision. Moving into a new home already involves enough work and stress, and you can make them feel relaxed and confident in their decision to move into your community. This is a better alternative than dropping a list of rules and regulations.

Provide Useful Information. The spectrum of your residents' previous locations is vast and diverse. Some may simply be transitioning from a nearby neighborhood, while others might embark on a significant relocation journey spanning the country's length. Additionally, you may have residents arriving from outside the country, navigating an international move's unique challenges and experiences. It is helpful to provide information such as:

- Location of amenities
- Map identifying local businesses
- Management office contact information: email, phone, text, QR code, etc.
- Process to submit service requests

- Utility companies and contact information

- Trash pickup day

- Local restaurants

- Entertainment venues

- Schools and playgrounds

- Neighborhood programs

Maintenance Procedures. Every home, whether rented or owned, requires maintenance work occasionally. While we all hope maintenance work is kept to a minimum, everyone must know how to properly submit a service request for work required in their apartment. No matter the job, it is helpful for everyone to have an organized system for taking care of such things.

Operational Procedures. Your occupants must know regularly scheduled cleanings, inspections, safety features, etc. To maintain your community certain things and preventative maintenance needs need to be done to uphold the value of your community. Your residents need to be aware of the system in place to maintain their homes without any surprises so that your building is well-kept, no one is caught off guard, and your occupants are happy.

Rules and Regulations. Now that you've covered all the essential information that would be considered welcoming and helpful for the occupants, they must also be aware of the procedures, rules, and regulations. Be clear and concise. Make it simple and appear important to the reader. These are things that should not be glossed over but read and understood.

Communicating this vital information and helping your residents understand expectations is excellent customer service. Providing your occupants with the best welcoming information packet will keep everything running smoothly and everyone happy. And your residents will have an easier time adjusting to life in their new home.

3: SAFETY & LIABILITY

How to Prevent Falls During the Winter

In climates that experience cold, snowy, and icy winters, the risk of slipping and falling outdoors is higher than in the warmer months. Between the snow and ice and the harsh winter winds blowing debris, there are increased dangers for anyone walking outside. If a renter or their guest falls on your property, you will be financially liable for any injuries. So, mitigating these risks and reducing the chance of falls is important. Doing weekly, monthly, quarterly, and annual inspections will help you identify potential liability issues, and you can address the items before someone gets hurt. Regularly scheduled preventative maintenance will minimize risks and add to your excellent customer experience for your residents and guests.

Check All Your Railings

Have your maintenance technician inspect all the hand railings on staircases and decks throughout your building or community. Ensure all railings are stable, can hold a lot of weight, and can be easily gripped even when wet. Also, look for areas that don't currently have a railing but could benefit from installing one, like tight corners or anywhere with a steep drop-off.

Clear Debris Daily

Make sure to assign someone to walk around the interior and exterior of your property every day of the year. Outdoors, cover green spaces, playgrounds, garbage areas, parking lots, and drives. The indoor check should include hallways, stairwells, elevators, amenities, and public bathrooms. Any debris, whether fallen tree branches, garbage, or anything blocking hallways, stairs, walkways, or driveways, should be removed immediately. Having a company on contract that can come anytime heavy debris needs to be moved with special equipment is also a good idea.

Clean Walkways and Parking Lots

After it snows, you must shovel all walkways and remove the snow from the parking lots. Likewise, you'll need to scatter ice removal products on walkways and parking lots after ice storms. Also, cold weather can be tough on concrete and asphalt, causing lifting, cracking, crumbling, and holes. So routinely check your walkways and parking lots for damage because this damage can be a tripping hazard or cause damage to vehicles. If you find any concrete and asphalt damage, immediately fix it or section off the area, so people cannot access those areas.

Emergency Preparedness

Typical emergency situations, in property management lingo, cover "fire, flood, or blood." Take a look at the headlines for the last 30-60 days; most of our country has suffered from some disaster or emergency situation: wildfires, hurricanes, earthquakes, tornadoes, bomb threats, renegade shooters, and pandemics. One of the duties of a property management company and its staff is to have a contingency plan in case of an emergency.

As property managers, what should we do? We must educate our staff about possible situations and how to respond to them. We should also include sample emergencies in our policy and procedure manuals and share a list of emergency contacts.

FEMA has leaders and regional offices around the country. Become familiar with the office closest to you. FEMA stands for the Federal Emergency Management Agency, an agency of the U. S. Department of Homeland Security. Their customer service number is 1-800-621-3362, and their website is https://www.fema.gov. A map of the United States shows which states are in which regions can be accessed by visiting https://www.fema.gov/regional-contact-information. This site also gives one access to flood maps. For the addresses and telephone numbers of the Emergency Management Agencies by state, visit https://www.fema.gov/emergency-management-agencies. The National Emergency Training Center is a subsidiary of FEMA. They teach courses on how to minimize the impact of disasters and emergencies.

Other "readiness resources" to have on your list should include:

- **Power outage**. Have the names and numbers of local electric supply companies.

- **Road closures**. Contact information for your state's Department of Transportation.

- **Water**. Numbers of the city or private water providers for sewer-related emergencies such as broken water mains, fire hydrants, water service lines, or sewer backups.

- **Cable, Phone, and Internet Service**. A list of local companies with phone numbers and websites.

- **Gas**. Local companies with numbers and websites.

- **Public Safety**. 911 and non-emergency numbers for police and fire departments.

- **American Red Cross**. http://www.redcross.org/get-help

- **Your County Department of Emergency Management**.

- **Your County Department of Public Health**.

- **Your State Department of Emergency & Military Affairs**.

You can also download a guide provided by the U. S. Department of Homeland Security at **Ready.gov** called **Protecting Your Family and Your Home, an Emergency Preparedness Guide**.

4: Unusual Amenities & Subleasing

Laundry Rooms, Pet Options, and Other Amenities, Oh My!

With the increase in renters, the real estate market has become more competitive. To give your community an edge, consider upgrading your features. A great way to give your apartments a competitive advantage in the market is to offer unique amenities rather than your competition's standards. Here are some ideas for unique amenities to consider that will attract new residents and increase retention.

Community Garden. Installing a community garden is incredibly cost-effective and attractive to residents, especially millennials who love to garden. You can include a community garden plot as part of the rent or allow residents to rent space if they desire. In any case, you'll be surprised by how many people will love this amenity.

Happy Hour. A great way to utilize your communal space is to offer a weekly happy hour. You can offer craft beer or wine tastings for your residents to purchase or just enjoy. Happy hour will give people a place to go where they can mingle with their neighbors and feel comfortable in the communal space.

Children's Area. Whether you add an outdoor playground or an indoor playroom, potential renters will love to see child-friendly amenities. Most apartment dwellers do not have enough chances to get their kids out to play and meet neighborhood kids, but adding these amenities gives them a strong sense of community.

Fitness Classes. Consider adding fitness classes if you have a fitness area, a large common room, or a pool. Whether you offer Yoga, Pilates, or water aerobics, your residents will love that they can get fit on site without buying an expensive gym membership. Fitness classes are another great way to build a sense of community and help your residents meet their neighbors.

All these amenities are inexpensive and easy to implement, no matter what type of community you have. These amenities will attract new residents and help foster a sense of community among your existing residents, making them worth the investment.

Subleasing

Why Your Leases Need a Vacation Rental and Subletting Clauses

From time to time, it's a good idea to review your lease agreements and update them as necessary. One clause that has become more important recently is about subletting, including, but not limited to, vacation rentals. With the growing popularity of crowd-sourced vacation rentals through websites like Airbnb, FlipKey, and VBRO, you, a property management professional, must ensure you and your property are protected.

What Is Subletting?

Subletting is when a resident finds someone else to cover their lease requirements. The other person moves into their space temporarily and pays the renter a fee. Often this is done when a renter needs help to complete the terms of their lease. They may move, lose their income, or require a larger space. With vacation rentals, your residents could make a profit on your rental.

Why You Need to Address Subletting

Subletting directly impacts your business. There are both pros and cons to allowing subletting. Pros include keeping your homes occupied when residents have to leave temporarily, reducing unexpected vacancies, and ensuring rent is paid on time. The cons include losing control over who lives on your rental as you will not screen these individuals. Whether you choose to allow subletting or not, since it impacts you and your rental, it is essential to include it in your lease.

How to Address Subletting in A Lease

There are many things you'll want to address when drafting your subletting clause, including:

1. State clearly whether subletting is allowed.

2. If allowed, outline the subletting screening process and any associated fees.

3. Identify the amount of notice required from the resident before allowing a sublet.

4. State conditions on subletting, including duration of the sublet.

5. Process on dealing with lease violations and damages during the sublet.

6. Detail restrictions on home-sharing platforms like Airbnb.

How you decide to structure your subletting depends on the business model of your community or management company. However, you are not required to allow subleasing. It is up to your discretion.

5: Online Agreements & Avoiding Late Payments

Cash/Check Rent versus Online Payments

With the expansion of technology, many new payment methods are available to property managers and residents. When exploring additional payment options, consider online payments and your standard cash or check payments. Both payment systems offer pros and cons, so consider the following before changing your payment system.

Cash/Check Rent Pros

- Cash and check payments are easier to track and require fewer bookkeeping processes.

- There is less risk of fraud or identity theft with accepting cash and check payments.

- There are no fees for accepting cash and check payments.

Cash/Check Rent Cons

- Cash payments, whether cash or check, are easy to lose. When you are running to the bank to deposit or trying to keep track of the payment within the office, you might lose the payment, which can be a bit of a financial hit.

- Cash payments are easier to steal. Though most staff are trustworthy, when you are going to the bank to deposit cash and checks, there is a risk of having your payments stolen.

- Most residents are not paid in cash, and checks are outdated with all the new payment systems available. So, having a cash payment system may be more difficult for your residents and even more costly if they must withdraw money from an ATM.

Online Payment Pros

- Online payments are extremely easy. Your residents sign onto a website and transfer the money.

- Online payments are speedy. Usually, within minutes of making the payment, you will have the money in your account.

- Online payments can be set up to automatically withdraw, which means your residents can pay their rent more efficiently and on time.

- When a resident struggles with bills, accepting online credit card payments means that the resident can pay rent even if they don't have the money in their bank account.

Online Payment Cons

- Many online and credit card systems have hefty processing fees, cutting your profit margins.

- Residents may dispute a payment transaction with their card company, which could cost you money.

- Online payments are prone to security leaks, so you must diligently monitor your transactions.

Both cash/check payments and online payments have their benefits and downsides. Deciding between the two comes down to measuring these pros and cons and considering which system is best for your unique residents. You can also consider introducing a hybrid system where you accept both forms of payment. The bookkeeping will be slightly more challenging with accounts payable coming from different sources, but your residents will appreciate the flexibility.

Avoid Late Payments

Late rental payments can be a burden for property managers. In addition to following up with overdue payers, your bill payments could be delayed, too. However, late rental payments are going to be something you will have to deal with from time to time. However, there are some processes you can implement to help reduce the number of late payments you receive.

Automate Rental Payment. Set up a system with automatic withdrawal. When rent is collected through direct deposit, it doesn't rely on renters remembering to send a check. Usually, you can set this system up with your bank. You'll just need to sign your renters up for the system.

Take A Variety of Payment Options. When you accept a variety of payment options, it makes paying rent easier. You can set up your payment system to accept checks, cash, and debit cards. You can even set up online auto-pay systems like PayPal, Apple Pay, or Square Cash.

Implement A Payment Reminder System. Sending out a notification to your renters that rent is due will help. A lot of the time, people forget to pay their rent on time. There are plenty of ways to do this effectively. You can send a text or email notification or deliver a reminder flyer every month. A simple, friendly reminder can make a difference.

Offer A Variety of Due Dates. Everyone has a different budget cycle. Some people get paid weekly, some monthly, and some per diem. If you offer a few different due dates, you can help your renters work around their income schedule. Consider offering weekly, monthly, or even quarterly. You can also shift the due dates from the first of the month to the middle of the month if it helps renters.

Ultimately, the best way to avoid late payments comes down to flexibility. Consider your current payment system and think about ways you can expand it.

6: PROTECT RESIDENT IDENTITIES

Landlords are required to adopt reasonable policies to prevent identity theft of their prospective, current, and past residents. There are rules and laws that have been put in place that must be followed by community owners and management company employees due to the handling of proprietary personal information obtained from residents. This policy should be included in your company's P&P manual.

Under the FTC's Red Flags Rule, which implements Section 114 of the Fair and Accurate Credit Transactions Act of 2003, a landlord may be considered a "creditor" based upon the FTC's current interpretation because it may collect past due rent. It relies on consumer reports requesting sensitive information, including Social Security Numbers and addresses. The Rule aims to keep sensitive information secure to prevent identity theft.

Identity Theft is defined as "fraud committed using the identifying information of another person."

A **Red Flag** is defined as "a pattern, practice, or specific activity that indicates the possible existence of Identity Theft."

Identifying Information is defined under the Rule as "any name or number that may be used to identify a specific person including name, address, telephone number, social security number, date of birth, government-issued driver's license or ID #, alien registration number, government passport number, employer or tax ID #, unique electronic ID #, computer IP address, or a routing code.

Identification of Red Flags. The following red flags may arise doing business in each of the following categories:

Notifications and Warnings from Credit Reporting Agencies

Red Flags

- Report of fraud accompanying a credit report.

- Report from a credit agency of a credit freeze.

- Report of an active-duty alert for an applicant.

- Activity that is inconsistent with the usual pattern of activity.

Suspicious Documents

- ID or card that appears to be forged or altered.

- ID or card on which a person's photo or physical description is inconsistent with the person presenting the document.

- Other documentation not consistent with customer information (such as a person's signature on a check appearing forged).

- Residency application that appears to have been altered or forged.

Personal Identification

- Identifying information presented that is inconsistent with the customer's other information (such as inconsistent birth dates).

- Identifying information presented that is inconsistent with other sources of information (ex., an address not matching an address on a credit report).

- Identifying information presented is the same as information shown on other applications that were found to be fraudulent.

- Identifying information presented that is consistent with fraudulent activity (such as an invalid phone number or fictitious billing address).

- The social security number presented is the same as another customer's.

- An address or phone number presented is the same as another person's.

- A person fails to provide complete personal identifying information on an application when reminded to do so (however, by law, SS#'s must not be required).

- A person's identifying information is inconsistent with the information that is on file for the customer.

Suspicious Account Activity or Unusual Use of Account

- Change of address for an account followed by a request to change the resident's name.

- Stop payment on an otherwise consistently up-to-date account.

- Mail sent to the resident is repeatedly returned as undeliverable.

- Notice to the landlord that a resident is not receiving mail sent by the landlord.

- Breach in the landlord's computer system security – unauthorized access to or use of resident's account information.

- Attempt to pay a full year's rent in advance.

- Rent payments begin being made by a third party.

Staff should take the following steps to detect red flags for a current resident.

- Verify the identification of the residents if they request information (in person, via telephone, via fax, via email).

- Verify the validity of the request to change the billing address temporarily or permanently.

- Verify changes in banking information given for billing and payment purposes.

- Obtain a reasonable explanation for rent payments coming from third parties.

In the event that your <u>staff detects</u> any identified red flags, it is recommended to take one or more of the following steps, depending on the degree of risk posed by the red flag:

Prevent and Mitigate

- Continue to monitor an account for evidence of identity theft.

- Contact the applicant or resident whenever suspicious circumstances dictate.

- Change any passwords or other security devices that permit access to resident information.

- Notify the program administrator for determination of the appropriate steps to take.

- Notify law enforcement; or

- Determine that no response is warranted under the circumstances.

Protect Resident Identifying Information

To further prevent the likelihood of identity theft concerning residents and applicants, take the following steps concerning internal operating procedures to protect resident and applicant identifying information.

- After holding files for the appropriate time, ensure complete and secure destruction of paper documents and computer files containing resident and applicant information.

- Ensure that office computers are password protected and that computer screens lock after a set period of time.

- Keep offices clear of papers containing consumer information.

- Except for applications for residency, do not request social security numbers.

- Ensure computer virus protection is up to date.

- Require and keep only the customer information that is necessary for landlord-tenant purposes.

- Keep all documents containing resident social security numbers, dates of birth, numbers on driver's licenses and other ID cards, consumer reports, and account numbers on resident financial institution accounts in a secure place, limiting access only to individuals with a business need for access.

Program Administration

The program administrator, a designated staff member, or a member of upper management should periodically review and update the company policy to reflect changes in the risks of identity theft to residents and applicants. In doing so, consider the prevalence of identity theft in the general multi-family community throughout your state, changes in identity theft methods of detection and prevention, and changes in the business arrangements with other entities your company does business with. If warranted, then update the policy.

The designated program administrator is responsible for the following:

- Ensure appropriate training of the office staff on the policy.

- Review any staff reports regarding the detection of red flags.

- Implement the steps for prevention and mitigation of identity theft.

- Determine which steps should be taken in particular circumstances.

- Consider periodic changes to the policy.

Service providers should also perform the activity with reasonable policies and procedures designed to detect, prevent, and mitigate identity theft risk. By contract, you may want to consider that service providers have such policies and procedures in place and that they review and report any red flags to staff.

Section 2: Seasonal Savvy

8: Spring Ideas

Spring Preparation & Maintenance Tips

Spring has finally arrived, and with the end of the harsh winter weather, it's time to do some spring cleaning, which can help improve your community, increase retention, and help attract new renters. Keep your properties in excellent condition to create a positive first impression on prospective residents. It also helps your current residents to be proud of residing in your community. Get your staff together and make your plan.

Spring Cleaning. Spring cleaning is not only for your buildings and grounds. It is also the perfect time to clean and organize the offices and maintenance shops. Spring cleaning applies to your models as well. Perhaps it is time to add new accessories to the model and offices and open the blinds to let the sunshine in. Clean the blinds, carpets, and, if needed, upholstery of the model and office furniture. Make sure everything looks and smells fresh and clean. Ensure surfaces look clean and free from grit, grime, and sticky residue.

File Cleaning. In the office, if you still need to do so, archive your old files to make room for new files. If you are HUD Financed, HUD Insured, a Project Based Voucher Community, LIHTC, etc., confirm that your HUD, state, and local program-related forms are the most recent. Dispose of the old forms to minimize confusion. Confirm that you are current on HUD policies, including the Notice of Occupancy Rights under the Violence Against Women Act. Don't forget to update your utility allowances and rent and income charts. Most of the utility updates "UAs" are out now, and HUD charts are pending publication at any time; keep an eye out for them. Also, check with your state regarding allowances for self-certifications which could save you a lot of time and money!

Aesthetics Matter. Use the natural laws of attraction to increase your traffic and rentals. You want to show the world that your community is well put together and cared for. It's important to remember that we are in the business of managing perceptions, and how you take care of your community indicates to the public how you will take care of them as residents.

Clean All the Common Areas. During the winter, people typically spend more time indoors so that things can get dirty in the common areas. Consider shampooing all the carpets to clean up any dirt and mud that may have been tracked. Also, wash any windows, clean the furniture, dust the light fixtures, and anything else that needs to sparkle. This is also a great time to check all the furniture and appliances in common areas to ensure they don't need repair.

Clean Up Your Landscaping. The exterior of your property is as important as the interior when it comes to attracting new renters. So, take some time to clean up all the landscaping around your property, including removing the debris from your garden beds, sweeping the sand and salt off your sidewalks and parking lot, and cleaning your gutters. This is also a great time to plan some new additions to your landscaping, so keep those in mind while you are picking up.

Clean Up Your Pool or Hot Tub. If you have a pool or a hot tub on site, spring is the perfect time to clean it and prepare the water for the summer pool opening. Call a pool professional to clean the filters and the water and ensure the perfect chlorine balance. Clean the decks, fences, furniture, changing rooms, and restroom areas.

Basic Indoor Maintenance. Beyond cleaning, take the time to do some basic essential indoor maintenance. Replace your air filters, check all the batteries on your smoke alarms, replace burned-out lightbulbs, and test your air conditioning system to ensure no issues. Check all the caulking and seals around windows and doors, which can get damaged in winter.

If you follow these essential tips and ensure that your property is compliant, fresh, and clean, you'll attract more residents, and it will be easier for them to rent come the busy spring rental season. These tasks are simple and can be done when the weather improves. So, make sure you get everyone on board and get to cleaning!

Spring Curb Appeal

Within seven seconds, we typically know if we like something, at least when it comes to first impressions. When it comes to your community, these first impressions mean a whole lot and can positively or negatively impact your occupancy and rent value. Your curb appeal significantly impacts first impressions more than many people may realize. Outstanding curb appeal will fare better than one with little to no curb appeal. Adding seasonal aspects to the landscape and grounds is a cost-effective way to ensure you stand out in the market.

Many "spring spruce-up" options are available depending on budget, availability, time, and planning. Here are a few simple and inexpensive ideas.

Quick Spring Spruce-Up

Plants and Flowers. First and foremost, spring is all about rebirth, and one sort of rebirth, in particular, is plants. Spring is all about color, which also rings true for your curb appeal. Using flowers and flower beds that really embrace the yellows, oranges, pinks, greens, and purples of the season can make your community stand out in a festive and totally "spring" way. Anything that adds a bit of color to the overall landscape brightens your community experience. These may seem like minor changes, but they are incredibly impactful in creating a gorgeous backdrop for your community.

- New trees

- Hedges

- Simple flowers

- Flowerpots and hanging baskets

- Fresh mulch that is or is not colorful

Lawn Refresher. Next, beautiful flowers should not rest on a dead lawn and brown grass backdrop.

- Rake dead leaves and plants, trimming dead wood, and picking up sticks will make a big difference.

- Put down some grass seed as needed to cover bare spots.

- Trim hedges.

- Edge sidewalks.

- Remove weeds.

Exterior Mini-Makeovers. Lastly, exterior surfaces can take a hit during the winter, mainly if your community is in a snowy climate. Weather effects can leave things looking dingy and dull, requiring you to refresh your exteriors.

- Power wash building siding, doors, and sidewalks.

- Touch up paint in any areas that have peeled or been damaged on the buildings and fencing.

- Paint a quick refreshed coat on doors and exteriors.

- Touch up signage or create new ones.

- Repaint parking lots.

Outdoor Lighting. Outdoor lighting can also really work the magic on your community.

- Light up all the areas of your community you'd like to highlight to make it bright and inviting.

- Mark special lighting to feature curb appeal on rainy days or at night-time.

- Signage should be well-lit, as it will allow those passing by to notice your name.

Spring Seasonal Staging

Residence staging is the one real opportunity to wow a prospect, so it should be taken seriously. It doesn't need to be costly to stage a residence effectively, and the reward comes quickly when you see touring prospects light up at the thought of calling your community home.

Staging can be catered to any season, and it gives your community a festive and fun appeal that touring prospects sincerely appreciate. Consider some of these ideas as the seasons change and holidays approach.

Spring & Summer Demonstrations

Spring and summer are the two most popular times of the year when folks are looking for a new community to join. In the fall, many are preparing for winter. In the winter, many find that the weather makes a move more complex, so they wait for spring and summer for the easiest transition to a new space. What this means for property management teams is that staging is most important in these seasons, and you'll want to take advantage of what the season has to offer in order to attract these prospective residents to your community above all others.

The most important thing to remember and consider when staging residences for spring or summer leases is the temperature in the space. When you're touring the actual residence, the prospective occupant will be leasing or viewing a staged model for show; keep control of the thermostat. Chances are, those coming to tour your spaces during this time of year will be dressed for the outdoor weather, which means a lot of shorts, sandals, tank tops, and other breezy cool clothing options.

What you don't want is to have these prospective residents stepping in from the warm outdoor air into an icebox, as this will make them uncomfortable and unable to focus fully. However, you also don't want the space to be uncomfortably hot for the same reason. An excellent way to set the temperature is to ensure it's between 70- and 75 degrees Fahrenheit, making it cool and comfortable compared to the outside. If the cooling is turned off in the unit, make sure to turn it on about an hour before the scheduled visit to give the space time to reach a comfortable temperature.

Another thing to consider outside is the lawn, especially the weeds and grass that tend to thrive in early summer weather but suffer at the latter end. If it's early in the year, ensure the grass has been sufficiently cut and the weeds pulled from any flower beds or around the property area.

If it's later and the grass has begun to turn brown and dry, give it a little water if the weather permits. Give it the best chance to look lush and healthy once again. A well-maintained outside will set the stage in perspective residents' minds of what they can expect when they walk through the door.

Spring Ideas for Your Residents and Renewal Gifts

Spring has sprung, and your residents are ready to leave their winter doldrums behind. Here are a few things you may wish to consider letting your residents do for spring cleaning and beautification of their apartment homes:

Container Gardening. If your community does not have a community garden, perhaps you can allow residents to grow their vegetables and flowers in appropriate containers on their patios and balconies. Appropriate containers would be ones that have a tray or dish beneath the pot to collect the overflow of water. We have probably all had a visit from a downstairs resident complaining that their upstairs neighbor watered their outdoor plants, and the water dripped onto their patio below. Set up a policy to explain planters' types, sizes, and approved placement. For example, no large concrete planters will be allowed on balconies for safety reasons, and no pots or planters are to be placed on railings.

Spring Organizing Ideas. Many retail stores now supply nothing but cleverly designed furniture and gadgets to make the most efficient use of space in any room or closet. Consider the following for spring organizers that can also be given as a renewal gift:

- Install a closet organizer.

- Over-the-door hanging organizers hold shoes, makeup, and jewelry.

- Stacking baskets hold books, magazines, folded clothes, etc.

- Murphy beds fold up against the wall when not in use.

- Some tables have tops that fold up against the wall.

- Sleeper sofas can serve as additional sleeping space for guests.

Painting Ideas. Allowing residents to have a painted accent wall is not new but still popular. Try choosing a handful of "approved" colors and let them choose one. If it's renewal time, have the maintenance technician do the painting for them. Painting a headboard on the wall instead of having a real one is cute and a space saver. If the front door to their apartment looks a little tired, give them a freshly painted front door to greet the world.

Room Dividers. It's easy to change and update a room for spring with free-standing room dividers. They can be used effectively in studios or one-room apartments. They can be strategically placed to screen the view when the front door is opened. They can also be placed to create a faux wall dividing living spaces or to screen off a kitchen or bathroom area. Lightweight folding screens are the best as they can be put up, moved, or taken down and stored easily.

Blinds and Curtains. Today, most apartments have some type of blinds already installed at the windows; however, some residents may also wish to hang curtains or drapes. You might choose a type of drapery or curtain rod and make it standard for all apartments so that those wishing to have curtains may, as long as they choose the type that works with the existing rods.

Wall Hangings. If you don't allow nails in your walls, consider giving a move-in gift that includes wall hangers for adhesive and removable pictures at move-out time. If you do allow nails, keep a picture hanging kit in the office to loan out to the residents. It should include a laser level, a small hammer, a pencil, measuring tape, and a variety of small nails, hangers, and wires.

Faux Windows and Murals. Not all apartments have great views. Why not allow residents to hang removable wall murals and faux windows on their walls? Find out who supplies them in your area or online and make that information available to your residents. Put one up in the bathroom of the clubhouse or fitness center to use as an example. Bring in the best light from the windows you already have and offer window cleaning – inside and out - at renewal time.

Floor Coverings. Spring cleaning back in the day would include taking the rugs outside for a good beating over the clothesline. Today, offer your residents a free carpet cleaning at renewal time. If it's not renewal time, see if your carpet cleaning vendor will offer a discount to your residents that call him directly for a cleaning. Consider giving them a voucher at move-in for a free carpet cleaning to be used anytime during the lease. Remind your residents that some throw rug backing can discolor vinyl flooring.

Retractable Screen Doors. Everyone wants to open the doors and windows when the nice spring weather arrives. Most communities do not allow the installation of permanent screen doors. The exteriors are nicer when they stay looking new and uniform in appearance. Consider allowing residents to purchase their own retractable screen doors that mount on the frame. Perhaps you can pick out a few good types and install them easily to suggest to those who want them. Check your local big box stores for samples and pricing.

Spring Events

Host resident events and invite guest speakers to speak to residents on ways to beautify their apartments (within your lease requirements) and provide crafts and demonstrations to make their apartments their homes. They can offer new ideas & inspiration to you and your residents while bringing your residents together for a community event. You might find such speakers among your various vendors at no cost to the property. For example, your floor and window covering company may have a decorator that would assist you by providing ideas. The owner of your painting company can give out brushes and color samples. Your landscaper might have someone who could bring in sample potted plants and a variety of pots that could be used for door prizes. Just be sure, in advance, that their ideas will be allowed in your community!

Easter Egg Hunt. Perfect for the little ones or everyone in your community, celebrating the spring season is a great idea. It can really get residents out and engaged with one another and attract passersby with the fun everyone is having. The eggs can be filled with change or small candies and hidden all around your community area!

Memorial Day Picnic. A patriotic Memorial Day picnic can allow your residents to have a great time getting out and shaking off that cooped-up feeling they've had during the cool winter and early spring seasons. The picnic can be open to residents and families or open to the public, and this can be a wonderful way for everyone to get out, socialize, and engage.

9: Summer Ideas

Enhancing Your Residents' Summer

Six Ways to Help Your Residents Reduce Air Conditioning Costs This Summer

Electrical bills in the summertime can be extremely costly, especially in particularly hot summers, where the air conditioning must run more often. Helping your residents save money on air conditioning has multiple benefits. It helps maintain lease renewals and keeps them cool and happy. Here are six ways you can help reduce air conditioning costs this summer.

Repair and Seal All Your Ductwork. The first thing you can do is check all the ductwork around your rental. Even a small duct leak can cause a loss of 25-30% of the air flow. Meaning it takes more energy and cooler settings to reach desired temperatures.

Apply Solar Film to Your Windows. Solar film added to windows blocks 60-70% of heat and sun. Solar film is also extremely cost-effective, averaging between $4-$6 a square foot, and has a lifespan of 10-15 years. If you are really concerned about price, you can just install it on windows that receive a lot of direct sunlight.

Change Your Air Filters. Dirty and clogged air filters can reduce the flow of air, making your HVAC system work harder to cool spaces. Changing all your air filters every six months can help keep the air flowing quickly and reduce your air conditioning from overworking. This will save electricity, which saves your residents money.

Repair or Replace Air Conditioning Units. Air conditioners today save 30-50% on electricity than air conditioners installed 15 years ago. If your air conditioning systems are older, it may be time to upgrade to more energy-efficient models. Though this will require a larger initial investment, the savings down the line for both you and your residents are worth every penny.

Plant Shade Trees. Planting trees around your community can help keep your building cool. Look for areas where there is a lot of direct sunlight hitting your building. Plant leafy trees to offer protection against the sun naturally with shade. Trees are very affordable and can reduce energy use by an average of 30% over the summertime.

Encourage Residents to Set Thermostats At 78°F. Though everyone has different temperature preferences, 78°F is the optimal temperature to keep air conditioning. Each degree lower than 78°F increases energy use by 6-8%. Let your residents know that just a few notches on their thermostats can save them a lot of money.

Summer Event Ideas

As summertime rolls around for your community, it's time to start thinking about the activities you could plan to bring your community together. For the summer months, a community-wide cookout for both residents and management is a great way to build relationships and encourage fun experiences on your property by holding a summer event for all ages.

Throw a Theme Party. Leave a box out for residents to suggest a desired theme. Then, you can either vote or just pick the one you like the best. Reward the resident whose theme was picked with a gift card to encourage participation. You could make this a regular event if you want to keep the fun going throughout the year.

Plan a Back-to-School Block Party. Many kids and families might be ready for one last hurrah before they return to the busy schedules that the school year brings.

Outdoor Movie Night. Get a projector and a screen and show a family flick outside. You can even just use a white sheet taped to the side of your building as a homemade screen. This is a fairly simple and inexpensive activity idea that can be done monthly throughout the summer. It will become something that many in the community look forward to as they build friendships and spend time enjoying the community and other residents.

End-of-Summer Tag Sale. Invite crafty residents to display and sell their homemade treasures during this sale and publicize the event.

Residents would need to register and reserve a table in advance, which the community would provide. It will allow the public to check out your community in fun and new ways. Your residents will appreciate the earned income, plus it will get you active in the community. Offer food or contact a local food truck to see if they would like to participate.

Bake Sale or Yard Sale. These types of sales help get residents out and working together while building organic relationships and a sense of community spirit. Have community members use open communal spaces to display and sell their wares. Others not looking to sell can browse and see what is being offered.

Stargazing Party. Put out telescopes and binoculars for people to sit back, stare at the skies, and relax.

Outdoor Book Club. In a common area within the community, host a book club in the evenings where residents go to discuss the book at hand with light snacks and beverages each member brings in. The beauty of this activity is that it can be brought indoors into an interior communal space for the changing of the season or inclement weather.

Take up a Local Project. Planting gardens, cleaning up communal spaces, or other service projects are another great way to bring the community together for the summer. The projects help to get everyone together while also giving residents an activity they can be truly proud of when they're all finished.

Fourth of July Block Party. A block party with music, games, activities for kids, and the grill going all day can really make your community the fun and inviting place, you want it to be. The block party can be open to all and even finish off with sparklers and ice cream to celebrate the nation's birthday!

Cookouts. If it's summer, it's time for a cookout. Here are some great ideas to consider when planning a community cookout:

- **Potluck Style.** Doing the cookout potluck style helps bring every community member into the fold and gives them a way to show off their cooking skills or party-planning talents. Invite community members to make and bring their most prized dish, favorite game, or some event prizes, and see how it inspires everyone to get involved.

- **Organize the Layout.** Having a community committee to help organize the layout and map out where all the activities will be taking place within the community. Organize a team that can use the map to determine how the final cookout layout will look.

- **Fun Activities.** Various fun activities will involve families of all types and sizes. Get everyone to have fun together and enjoy all the delicious food everyone has to offer. Frisbee, games, slip and slides, races, face painting, coloring stations for the kids, and other fun summer-friendly things to do will be a big hit with staff and residents alike!

- **Get Playlist Input.** No summertime cookout is complete without a great summer playlist. Getting suggestions from the community is a great way to ensure the playlist will have a little something for everyone.

Community activities help build that organic sense of true community that is important to management and residents. Summertime is the perfect time to embrace the power of community activities!

10: FALL IDEAS

Fall Community Updates and Fun

Autumn is undeniably a beautiful season. The leaves are changing colors on the trees, the oppressive summer air is replaced with crisp fall breezes, and those looking for a new place to live will be on their search before winter sets in. When you're trying to attract prospective new residents to your community, you'll want to take advantage of autumn's beauty. How can you create autumn curb appeal? Here are some ideas to "fall" in love with every year.

Fall Clean Up. The beauty of autumn looks best with well-maintained and kept landscaping.

- Rake leaves
- Mow lawn
- Keep edges clear

Out with the Old, In with the New. A warm welcome awaits you.

- Replace summer flowers and landscaping with fall flowers and accents.

- Add a few hanging baskets.

- Plant bushes where needed; replace those that have died.

- Deadhead plants.

- Clean out flower beds.

Fall Décor. Invest in a wreath or two can also make your community more inviting. If you have a community office space, create that stellar first impression to make people feel welcome. A fall wreath hanging on the door brings that seasonal beauty right to your doorstep and invites prospective residents inside in a positive way to learn more about becoming a member of the community you've built.

Lighting. Daylight will decrease during the winter months so during the fall do a nighttime light check throughout the community. Replace burned out lightbulbs.

Fall Staging

Just because cooler weather is coming in, doesn't mean you're going to stop giving tours! If you're attracting new prospective residents to your community, some of them are going to want to stop by to check it out for themselves, and this will require a little home staging. By staging the residence, you're showing them a better picture of their potential lifestyle once they move in. The fun part is there are some clever ways you can do this that are perfect for the fall and winter seasons.

First and foremost, you're going to want to keep the temperature down. While the chill outside may seem like the perfect reason to crank up the furnace, remember that people will be coming to visit while wearing a jacket or a coat. While they're touring the residence, they don't want to have to carry their jacket, leave it somewhere, or overheat in it, so you want to keep the home comfortable for them. A good rule of thumb is to keep the temperature of the residence at around 60- to 65- degrees Fahrenheit.

For decorative touches, use an autumn color palette. Outdoors is easy, with a few pumpkins, some seasonal blooms, and leaf décor turns the community into a festive and fall-friendly space.

Indoor touches in autumn colors for vases, blankets, napkins on a set table, or hand towels in shades of gold, russet, deep red, and forest greens create an instant feeling of fall.

Additionally, warm textiles such as area rugs and blankets in plush and warm fabrics in fall-friendly colors really add cozy to the demonstration. Draping a thick chunky blanket over a sofa can make touring prospects imagine the space as their own comfortable sanctuary.

Give Thanks to Your Residents

Thanksgiving is right around the corner and what better time to thank your residents? Holidays are great backdrops to use for working on resident retention rates at your communities. Thanksgiving may even be one of the best opportunities. It's a time of sharing and caring and can involve your entire community.

Show that you care with a message. A simple and very affordable solution for you to show you care is to simply write a thank you note. Create a short message to mail out or deliver to your residents in the days leading up to the holiday. It will make a positive and lasting impression on your residents.

Have a gathering with a Thanksgiving theme for those residents interested in getting together. Not everyone has family nearby, and breaking bread and sharing a turkey dinner with neighbors can be a great substitute. Supply the cooked turkey (or allow a vendor to show their "thanks" by supplying one) and ask residents to bring the side dishes and desserts. Prior to eating, give those present the opportunity to express thanks for whatever is important to them. What a great way to create a sense of community! Remember that the more often people get together like this, the more likely they will remain at the same location.

Thanksgiving is another good time to gather a group of residents to become volunteers to work at a homeless shelter, hospital, or soup kitchen to serve Thanksgiving meals to those less fortunate than ourselves. It costs nothing, and the value to everyone involved cannot be measured. Most often, people just want to feel appreciated. Give them something to feel good about!

11: WINTER IDEAS

Wonderful Winter Updates and Fun

Unless you live in the deserts of Arizona, your community will most likely have to prepare for winter weather in the coming months. Even in winter, curb appeal can still set you apart from the competition and attract prospects. The following are a few seasonally appropriate tips and reminders to assist you and your staff members in preparing for winter.

Snow Removal by Staff and Vendors. Vendor contracts must be negotiated in advance for snow removal, and supplies must be in stock on-site before bad weather hits. Some snow removal companies do nothing but snow removal, but others do landscape or other services during other times of the year. Interview both kinds and seek out the best pricing, but always ask for and follow up with their references.

Sanding/Salting/Snow Melt Application. Stock up on snowmelt supplies now before you need them, and review with maintenance and groundskeepers how their daily tasks will change for winter.

Driveways. Your snow removal vendor should be able to move snow for you, but they can't always take it away. Make sure you tell them where they can put the excess snow on site if they have to stack it up.

Sidewalks. Resident safety is always at the top of the list year-round. In winter months, ensure your walkways are clear and slip free and that handrails are secure. Sidewalks may need to be cleared several times a day.

Roofs and Carports. When snow falls continuously and cannot melt due to temperature, the weight of it can become dangerous. Ceilings can crack and fall in and carports can bend over or totally collapse from the weight of excess snow. If there is not a snow melting heat line built into the roofing or gutters, staff members may have to manually remove excess snow. Before it starts to snow, make sure gutters are cleaned of leaves and debris and that maintenance has the proper snow removal equipment in their maintenance shops: snow shovels, snow blowers, etc. Don't forget the icicles! As the snow melts and drips from rooftops and carports, it can refreeze, forming dangerous icicles. Icicles can become very long; if they fall from some height, they could hurt people or damage vehicles. Remove them when they are small before they have a chance to develop into deadly spears of ice.

Protection of Fire Risers and Sprinkler Systems. If you have ever had to be on "fire watch" overnight for a building that had pipes freeze and burst that affected the fire suppression system, you already know about the importance of preventing a freeze. Wrapped pipes and equipment room heaters can prevent freezing.

Carpeting and Mats at Building Entrances. Replace damaged floor mats now and budget to clean office carpets and interior hallway carpets more frequently. Daily maintenance may be necessary.

Your maintenance plan needs to be specific to your community. Plans will change from one location to the next. Walk your community now with your maintenance staff and create your maintenance plan together.

Winter Curb Appeal

Curb appeal is pretty simple during the spring and summer months, when you can use clean landscaping and flowers to draw the eye to your community from passersby on the road. Your curb appeal doesn't have to take a season off simply because Mother Nature may refuse to cooperate. There are things you can do to beautify your community, even during the coldest months of the year. In the winter, things get a bit more difficult, but not impossible. The following ideas are sure to improve your curb appeal during the cooler months of the year.

Keep it Clean.

- Rake fallen leaves.

- Keep the grass short, even if it's not growing as it was a couple of months earlier.

- A clean and seasonal look can draw the eye to your community and pique the interest of those passing.

Plants. Almost everything except the firs and evergreens will go dormant or die off in your landscaping. Keep some of these planted by your entrance and leasing office. You can strategically place holly in pots with red berries and poinsettias for color.

Merry and Bright. The winter months become a little more difficult, and it can be tough to keep your curb appeal as you'd like it with dirty grey snow, bare trees, and an icy look. However, this doesn't mean it's impossible. Incorporate light into all aspects of your community; on your signage, lights lining the sidewalks, twinkling lights in trees, and lights on the buildings themselves can allow your residences to be seen without much effort from all around outside. Lighting can also make your current residents happy by making them feel safer and more secure, so there is a double benefit!

Safety First. For the latter half of the winter season, you won't have the holiday decorations to draw visitors in, so you'll want to focus on your upkeep.

- De-ice all sidewalks, exterior steps, parking lots, and streets.

- Keep walkways and parking lots cleared from snow.

- Present a clean and well-put-together curb appeal for your community that communicates the type of care you put into your community.

Holiday Tours

While spring and summer are usually the prime times for attracting new prospective residents, plenty will be looking for communities around the holidays as well. Staging your community and models for tours around the holidays can be a fun and creative experience, and while you will enjoy getting into the spirit, it's important not to go too far. Be sure to select décor that appeals to all holiday traditions, so your visitors feel included. A few things not to do when staging your residences for the holidays include:

Don't Go Overboard Trying to Create Curb Appeal. Curb appeal during the holidays provides a lot of different directions, and a lot of ways to gain attention. A good rule of thumb to follow is to go simple and elegant. It's best to be understated than overdone. Too many yard decorations or lights can be off-putting, making the property look cluttered and possibly trashy.

Don't Wear Out Your Welcome. Scent, flavor, light, and sound can all be ways to make prospects feel at home and welcome in your community, but only when it's done well. Creating your welcome is easy, but using a mix of candles, potpourri, baked goods, air fresheners, and lots of warmth can have the exact opposite effect. Instead, keep it simple with a plate of fresh cookies and a bit of warm cider, or a single holiday-scented candle lit earlier in the room and put out to allow the lingering delicate aroma to take over. Also, avoid turning up the heat and remember that touring prospects will likely wear jackets or coats.

Don't be Overenthusiastic About Décor. A tree, pillows, place settings, curtains, rugs, and other pieces of décor should be chosen wisely. A good rule of thumb to follow is to leave it to small accents and let them do the legwork. Instead of a tree, small greenery candle holders will look more versatile and elegant. Instead of a holiday rug, a couple of accent pillows will do the trick.

Decorating your models and common areas for the holidays provides a fun way to allow your community's creativity to shine, but it's important not to go overboard and wind up turning prospects away.

New Year's Resolutions for Community Management Teams

Each new year is a new opportunity to improve your community, your engagement, and the experience you provide to your residents.

Update All Leases and Pet Policies. For many community management teams, leases grow out of date, pet policies are left with holes, and little is done about it. For this New Year's resolution, commit to updating your leases, creating great pet policies for pet-friendly communities, and showing residents that you're always on top of what they need.

Build Emergency Funds for Each Residence. All too often, when an emergency happens, community management teams can be left a bit lost. Rather than scramble to find the funding for repairs, ensure you have an emergency fund to cover every residence in your community. Repairs will be carried out faster and more effectively.

Make a Commitment to Network. There's a lot to learn from other community management teams, and a lot those teams can learn from you. This year make it a point to get out there, network with others in the industry and learn firsthand what you can gain from such a friendship and professional partnership.

Commit to Streamlining at Least One Process. Are you making multiple trips to the bank to deposit resident checks? Are you flipping between too many social media pages one after the other? This year make it a point to streamline at least one process and save yourself some time and money.

Holiday Events

How to Plan a Community Holiday Party for All Ages

The holidays are a great time to host a community party which will encourage residents to get to know each other as well as the community staff members. When planning a community party, you'll want to try to appeal to a wide range of audiences from families to seniors. But before you land on the party idea that's right for you, here are a few more things to consider:

Timing

There are many holidays celebrated throughout the month of December including Hanukkah, Christmas, and Kwanzaa. Remember to be inclusive of all your residents and plan the party around these celebrations when people will likely be spending time with family.

Since many people are traveling in middle-to-late December, the earlier the party, the better.

Consider if your guests are more engaged on weekdays or weeknights. Will a casual gathering after work get more attendance? Are people more energized on the weekends?

Budget

How much can you allocate to your holiday party? A small budget may mean you'll provide snacks or host an inexpensive activity like cookie decorating. A larger budget may mean you'll cater a meal and turn the party room into a winter wonderland. Keep track of the details needed to plan your party.

- Number of guests

- Food

- Drinks

- Decorations

- Activities

- Gifts

Though providing gifts is unnecessary, a small, branded item like a keychain, water bottle or bottle opener with your company or community logo can be a nice thank-you to residents for choosing your community as their home.

Activities

Anyone would be thankful for a catered meal, but if you want to take your party to the next level and create a memorable experience, don't forget to provide a few activities. You could even create multiple stations for different age groups.

If you're planning an elaborate party for families, you could hire a face painter or balloon artist. If that's out of your price range, there are lots of free holiday games and coloring pages online, and many other different activities that kids and adults would both enjoy.

Holiday Trivia

If you're catering to an adult crowd, holiday trivia is a great way to get residents to work together in teams. This version pulls from movies, songs, classic foods, and more, so it can appeal to a wide variety of interests. For example, can you name the state that grows the most Christmas trees?

Pin the Face on the Elf

This is a great one for kids and adults alike! Print out faces of popular celebrities or cartoon characters. Have everyone take turns being blindfolded and trying to place the face on the elf's body. Whoever gets it closest wins!

Guess the Carol

Who doesn't love a good holiday song? If you're having a karaoke party, or just have residents who love to sing, this is the game for you! Each resident needs a copy. Give everyone time to fill out the sheet, translating a string of emojis into a carol. For higher stakes, set a time limit. The person who gets the most answers right wins.

Cookie Decorating Party

Cookies are a holiday staple and a cookie decorating party can be a blast. Plus, it is super easy to organize. Simply choose a room with a lot of tables. Then lay out some pre-baked sugar cookies, a variety of frosting and icings, and a selection of candies. If you want, you can even do gingerbread houses. To take it up a notch have some hot cocoa, coffee, or other drinks available to go with the cookies. If sweets aren't your thing, you can also decorate Christmas ornaments or make Christmas cards. The best part is that this party works great for children and adults of all ages.

Holiday Movie Night

A holiday movie night is a great way for your residents to get together, keep cozy, and enjoy the season. Find a room with a ton of comfortable seating, and pick a holiday movie. You can also serve classic movie theater snacks like popcorn, candies, slushies, or a selection of holiday treats. The movie you pick should reflect your residents. If you have a community with a lot of families, choose something like "A Christmas Story," or "How the Grinch Stole Christmas." If you house a lot of younger singles, opt for something more adult, like "Elf" or "Love Actually." If you have older generations residing in your community, choose traditional Holiday movies such as "Miracle on 34th Street," or "It's a Wonderful Life."

Holiday Karaoke

If your community is known for throwing large, fun bashes, a karaoke party is perfect for you. Start by getting a karaoke machine or if you have the budget, hire a karaoke DJ, then offer a variety of classic Christmas songs and have your residents go for it! Make sure to serve food and drinks. Eggnog is a must at a holiday karaoke party to help get everyone in the spirit to sing. This idea can work for communities with families as well.

Show the Love for Valentine's Day

Your community should embrace a "love at first sight" sort of appeal to your potential residents and welcome home your current residents showing you care, and it should set you apart from your competition.

Love Notes for Your Residents

Love is in the air. Valentine's Day often brings out the best in people. When it comes down to it, it's a fun holiday without a lot of expense, time, or effort put on the line. There's no doubt that you want to celebrate this type of holiday with every one of your residents.

What you may not realize, though, is that using Valentine's Day as a backdrop, you can work on building your image, improving your overall brand, and ensuring better retention rates at your community. Why not turn things around and start creating an atmosphere that allows anyone and everyone to appreciate what you have to offer?

Love Note #1--Show You Care with a Message

Not everyone has a love for this holiday. You don't want to force it on them. However, a simple and very affordable solution for you to show you care is to simply write a thank you note. Sure, it may not seem like much, but for your residents, it matters. How many people send in their rental payments on time, never call you, and rarely ever even blip on your radar as a problem? You want to thank these people because they make your job easier. They often appreciate this type of simple communication that can send a message that's heartfelt.

If you have not done so previously, create a short message to mail out to your residents in the days leading up to the holiday. Say something simple like, "In the spirit of Valentine's Day, we want to say thanks." Doing this costs virtually nothing but makes a big and lasting impression on your residents.

Love Note #2-Throw a Party

You don't have to spend a lot of money, but you will brighten your residents' days and create loyalty when you invest in a small gathering for those interested. It does not have to have a romantic theme. Invite the kids to come along for the fun. Here are some simple tips to make it low-cost but enjoyable:

- Bring everyone together for a thank-you breakfast of just donuts and coffee. Keep it simple, invite everyone, and say thanks to him or her.

- Use Valentine's Day decorations to create a "we love you" campaign in the building.

- Ensure that everyone realizes that you appreciate each and every resident.

- If you have a larger space, welcome everyone for a pot-luck meal on the holiday itself.

- You supply the decorations, and basic food, and welcome everyone to bring a treat. This is an excellent way to bring people together.

- Ask your vendors to show their "love" for your community by providing the main dishes for your event.

- If you live in a warmer climate and the weather is decent, host a playground party for the kids. Encourage exchanging Valentines and chatting.

By doing this, you are not only building your brand as a fun, innovative place to live, but you are also giving people the ability to meet each other. The more often people get together like this, the more likely they are to remain at the same location especially when they have friends they like, know, and trust. It builds retention.

Love Note #3—Love is in the Air and on the Screen

If you have a community space with a television, schedule a 24-hour movie marathon with Valentine's Day-themed movies. All you need to do is provide the movie, popcorn, and refreshments. Invite all the residents to come in at some point during the movie marathon to watch their favorite romantic comedy. For fun, keep it going and have contests like the "funniest" pajama contests and other lighthearted contests. This event gives your residents an opportunity to take a break and come down and have some fun with their neighbors...building and nurturing friendships!

Love Note #4—Share the Love

There are many local centers and non-profits that would love to share in the love with your residents so why not rally your residents together to volunteer at a soup kitchen, a homeless shelter, or a hospital. Volunteering is ultimately about helping others and having an impact on people's well-being.

What better way is there to connect with your residents and the local community and give a little back? Volunteering brings together a diverse range of people from all backgrounds and walks of life. Both the recipients of your volunteer efforts and your residents can be a rich source of inspiration and an excellent way to develop loyalty. This is a completely free event, and the value is incredible to you and your residents and those who benefit from such a good deed.

Love Note #5--Create an Open Invitation

During the winter months, people are spending more time indoors. You may notice more frustrations and anxiety building up in many of these months. Yet, you can create a break from it by simply opening up the communication. Let Valentine's Day be a day to come and talk. Allow people to interact with each other in a simple gathering, or, welcome them to stop by the office and discuss their needs and ideas.

Creating a Valentine's Day theme for any type of gathering or retention process allows your residents to see just how much you really appreciate them. While you could give them expensive gifts or all of your time, most often, people just want thanks and to feel appreciated. Take the time to plan something small but ensure that the message of meeting your residents' needs is what comes through.

SECTION 3: AESTHETIC EXCELLENCE

12: YEAR-ROUND MAINTENANCE

Stay on Top of Your Maintenance

Staying on top of preventative maintenance is important to both cutting maintenance costs and keeping current residents happy. Knowing just how to stay on top of things can be somewhat difficult. There is a lot to consider, to remember, and to worry about when managing a community of any size, and these small problems can often slip through the cracks of your knowledge bank.

Keep Fully Staffed. There is nothing worse than waiting on the phone, in line or for an available person. Prospective residents become fidgety and frustrated. When you're short staffed or stretched thin, it can also be really difficult for your employees to ignore the strong feelings of frustration thrusted upon them. These feelings, no matter how well hidden they may be, will translate to your residents. This can cause current and potential residents to feel unwelcome, uncomfortable, and even anxious, which is exactly what you don't want.

Inspections. Holding regular inspections of your residences and community areas can really help you to stay on top of problems that may be occurring. During this time, you are given a way to investigate the soundness of various structures, hear any concerns residents may have, and arrange for solutions to be put in place. The regularity of the inspection process can allow you to always stay a step ahead!

Welcome Concerns. Encourage residents to bring any maintenance concerns to you right away to stay on top of your preventative maintenance. Provide contact information and respond promptly to let your residents know that they can always count on you to get the job done.

Keep Your Team Informed. Your maintenance team can also be a big help in keeping you on top of your preventative maintenance. Keep them informed and encourage them to investigate structures and keep repairs in mind. With an extra set of eyes working to keep things in working order, it will be easy to manage maintenance needs throughout the year.

Year-Round Preventative Maintenance Ideas for Your Property

Caulking Tiles. Prevent water damage in the bathroom and kitchen by caulking tiles on a regular basis. All it takes is a small amount of moisture or mold to get inside a crack in your tiles to cause a larger problem. While you are in the areas where water is most frequently used, also check for any leaks. Water leaks can cause damage immediately and can be very costly to fix.

Pest Prevention. This is important in both the winter and the summer. You can put traps and repellants for mice, bugs, and other pests that might want to make their home in your investment. Preventing them from coming in will save you a lot of hassle later.

Paint. There is nothing quite like a fresh coat of paint. It makes things look new and can also save you from other dangerous problems. Chipping and peeling paint can be a fire and choking hazard for small children. Check on paint often to avoid a dangerous situation.

Electrical System. Be sure to keep an eye on the electrical system on your property. A mouse might chew through a wire, or a wire might need to be replaced, and you won't be aware unless you check the box regularly. Residents have also tried to hook up things on their own, making dangerous connections where there shouldn't be any. Checking in often will avoid a potentially devastating outcome.

Air Filters. Keep the air in your spaces clean and fresh by replacing the air filters on a regular basis. Air filters collect all kinds of dust and mold. If they are not changed regularly, they will send dust and mold right back out into the air for everyone to breathe in again. This could cause sickness, allergic reactions, and more in your residents and employees. Proper maintenance is key.

Keeping up with your maintenance will save you from costly repairs in the future. You can keep an eye on what is going on, while also keeping everyone healthy and safe.

Avoid Patio Clutter

If you ever drive by an apartment building where the patios are a cluttered mess, you can see why it is a bad reflection of your property and how your unit should look. Clutter does not do anything for aesthetics, so help your residents understand that they need to keep their balconies clutter-free. Here are some ways to do that.

- Add patio restrictions to your lease agreements. Let new residents know that a cluttered patio is not ok, and management reserves the right to tell you that your patio is too cluttered. Have them sign something in the lease agreement that shows that they've read and understood the clause for future reference.

- Be specific about what is and what is not allowed on the patio area. Do you allow grills? Charcoal or gas? Do you allow kid pools? Do you allow pets to be left out on the balcony? Think carefully about the kinds of things you want on display for everyone driving past your building to see, and also about any safety or noise concerns.

- Be sure actually to enforce the policy. This one sounds like a no-brainer, but it is harder than it sounds. If one resident sees another resident's cluttered patio, they will think it is ok to do the same on their patio, and so the pattern goes. Actively enforcing your policy will keep the standards the same for everyone, and no one will take advantage of the rules.

- Offer an alternative storage solution. Do you have space in the basement to create storage lockers? Can you suggest a storage facility up the road? Maybe you could even make an agreement with another local business about offering your residents a discount to use their facility in exchange for free advertising.

- Make it into a contest. Award the resident with the nicest looking balcony with a gift card or some sort of prize. If it gets turned into a competition, you can get all the residents involved. Spruce it up to become a decorating contest for holidays or seasons to add more fun to the game.

Follow-Up After Maintenance

After a resident of your community has maintenance performed or a problem fixed within their home, follow up with them to show you care and reinforce your customer-focused community.

Maintenance is something to be expected within your communities, even if it can be an inconvenient experience for those who find themselves in need of it. Having a maintenance crew who are trusted and well-liked within the community can help to make maintenance less of a hassle, but a follow-up with your residents can create an even better experience.

Follow-up is as simple as a quick phone call to your resident and inquiring about their maintenance experience. Was the repair performed properly? Their satisfaction is a great deal to their overall experience of life in your community.

If a phone call isn't possible, you can also send a short e-mail asking the same questions and showing the same concern. An email only takes a few minutes to write up, and it can really make all the difference in showing your residents that you care. In these e-mails, you can also work to address other maintenance or repair concerns and stay on top of how people feel about your community.

13: CURB APPEAL & STAGING FOR DEMONSTRATIONS

Better Curb Appeal for Your Community

A lot of different elements are required to build a successful, sustainable, and fully occupied apartment community. Property managers must focus on everything from collecting rents and hiring employees to reviewing resident applications, maintaining the communities and beyond. In the busy day to day, there are areas that can be easily overlooked. Curb appeal happens to fall into the 'overlooked' category which leads to missed opportunities.

Home improvement shows continuously stress the importance of curb appeal for the sale of single-family homes; it's no different for multi-family residences. In order to hold true to our new commitment to make lasting first impressions, curb appeal is the first step.

No matter the location of the property, apartment communities can seem like an automatic draw for residents. But as more and more communities are built, standing out and getting noticed becomes more difficult and so much more important. Your website can be as slick and well designed as possible, but if the community no longer matches the photographs, or if the community itself doesn't really wow them, it will be harder than you might think to fill all of your apartments.

Paying attention to the curb appeal of an apartment community is an absolute must. Taking a closer look at this facet of facility management is well worth the effort and could have a big impact on future occupancy rates. Afterall, we want to make sure that each pathway keeps residents oohing and awing through their whole experience ending with saying or thinking, "This is home."

What Is Curb Appeal?

Curb appeal refers to the overall appearance of an apartment community when viewed from the street. Essentially, when someone drives by the community or pulls into the parking lot, everything they see from their vehicle is considered overall curb appeal. Everything from the parking lot to the landscaping and even the condition of the entrance, lobby and hallways represents curb appeal.

Great curb appeal and worn curb appeal can have a huge impact on the desirability of a property. If people arrive to tour the grounds and see trash, unkempt landscaping, junk piled up on balconies or patios, flaking paint, and other issues, they'll be less likely to rent an apartment than if they arrived at an immaculate, beautiful community.

Why Does Curb Appeal Matter So Much?

Our goal is to leave lasting impressions, and curb appeal falls into one of the paths to first impressions. Great curb appeal is also an indication to the prospect of how we not only take care of our property, but it is an indicator of how we will take care of them as residents. Without good curb appeal, you end up struggling to attract residents – no matter the condition of the interior apartments.

- Curb appeal is incredibly important for apartment communities and can help in numerous influential ways.

- Whether or not someone decides to rent at your community

- Provide value in the rent per apartment home

- Overall mood and morale of residents and onsite team

- Build a better brand identity

- Bolster community goodwill

Give Your Curb Appeal A Boost

When you want to attract residents, sell a long-term living experience instead of a one-year lease. It's important we recognize that the outside quarters are just as important as the inside because it starts from the moment they drive into your parking lot.

The better your curb appeal, the better experience you will have managing the community. But how do you go about improving curb appeal, exactly? It can initially seem like a tremendous amount of work, but the reality is that by just paying attention to a few key things, you can help build better curb appeal in your apartment community.

There are two steps to bolster your curb appeal to increase your rate of interest (ROI).

Community Management Review

The first step is a comprehensive community management review and assessment. Begin by standing back and looking at the whole property through the lens of a prospective resident. Look for anything that stands out and what might need to be fixed or changed.

Major Issues. Start by identifying potential major problems like peeling paint, damaged siding, and so on. Deal with the big issues first since they'll be the first things others see upon arriving at your community.

Grounds. Maintain the grounds well. Cut grass, edge sidewalks, trim hedges, and clean parking lots.

Décor. Small touches can help, too. Accent plants like shrubs or planters with bright flowers can help, and always be sure to add a few decorations for different holiday seasons.

Economical Curb Appeal Improvements

Maintaining the exterior of your community is crucial to your success. Luckily, improving curb appeal doesn't have to empty the bank account. Here are some simple, inexpensive ideas for your community.

Keep It Clean. The easiest and most cost-effective way to improve your community's curb appeal is to keep the property clean. Clear all the litter and debris from outdoor common areas every day. Check your property routinely to see if anything looks dirty or run down and clean it immediately. Even something as simple as cleaning the exterior of the entry door can freshen the look of a property. Don't forget to clean and buff door handles, light switches, and light fixtures. Buying or renting a power washer to clean the front area and façade once per season is a great idea.

Paint. Painting is a low-cost way to keep things looking new. Consider appealing color schemes or even fun ideas like an accent color for doors, trim, and banisters. A simple paint job can make your property look new and inviting.

Landscaping. A little landscaping can leave a lasting impression. Keep grass cut, trees pruned, flower beds weeded and watered, shrubs trimmed, and walkways edged and clear of debris.

Lighting. Exterior lighting does a few things for your community. First and foremost, it helps residents feel safer. Outdoor solar lights are very inexpensive and come in various styles, colors, and types. Something as simple as spotlighting signs or adding garden lights to your landscaping can really create an attractive space. Lighting should be consistent without any burnt bulbs or broken fixtures.

Signage. Ensure signs are in good condition and can be read. Temporary signs and flags should be straight, and balloons inflated with all old remnants of previous balloons and strings removed.

Hide Utilities. Utilities are necessary, but they can be very ugly. A great idea to increase curb appeal is to hide them behind landscaping or paint them so they blend in with the property. Keeping them from standing out will help your property look better.

Routine Maintenance & Preventative Maintenance Inspections. Keep everything repaired and in good working order. Regular inspections of the exterior of the property are easy to complete and could help you spot problems that need to be addressed. Whether it's painting, replacing shingles, or something else, it's vital to maintain your property for the best curb appeal. When arriving at your home, consider what you want to see, and then check to ensure your community lives up to your standards.

Community Effort. Ensure leases stipulate that residents can't leave garbage exposed outside the apartment, use their balcony or patio for storage, and maintain a well-kept appearance outside their apartment.

Investment Improvements for Impressive Curb Appeal

Extended Landscaping. A beautiful landscape really adds to the look of your community. However, between the costs of landscaping and maintenance, the costs can get out of hand quickly. These are a few simple ways to reduce the cost.

- Choose native vegetation plantings that do not require much attention and will grow without much maintenance.

- Focus on landscaping the areas seen most by potential clients, like the entry to the leasing office or along the street. These are the places you want to make the most impact.

- Make sure your community looks like a place where things are well-kept and extra steps are taken to ensure a comfortable and beautiful experience.

Decorative Accents. Some simple decorative accents can have a big impact. Upgrade the building numbers, add potted or hanging plants, or add molding and trim around the building entrances to make your community more inviting. Don't be afraid to get creative.

Modernize. A modern curb appeal will catch the eye, so make sure to update anything that requires updating in order to attract those passing by. This includes signage; if the signs are faded, paint or replace them.

Parking Lot. The most often overlooked part of the exterior of a community is the parking lot. However, you don't always have to have the lots repaved to keep them looking great. Repainting parking lines and space numbers every year can keep them looking fresh. A parking lot that features cracks, overgrowth, debris, or an overall "shabby" appearance, will make residents and potential residents think that this is what they're going to experience inside, too. Taking care of your lots will let residents and potential residents know you take care of your entire property.

The Importance of Staging Your Apartments & Homes

Whether you are in the business of residential leasing of apartments or single-family homes, the very first impression of our residents' experience may very well be the website or the front door to the office. The next experience is the second most important: the demonstration of your community, amenities, and models. Trends over the past couple of decades have proven that staging our properties is well worth the investment.

Various communities show vacant units or could showcase model units. Either option for any type of rental property is important for your business because it draws in your customers, showing them what living or staying in your community would be like.

For those that have models, there is much more control over the cleanliness, décor, and availability. Keeping this unit in tip-top shape with all the neutral décor, relatable furniture, and the latest upgrades is important.

Staging vacant units can be one of the most important steps you can take to enhance your customer's experience. It is fun, too. As you will see, many options exist to dress up your space to attract your residents.

Leading prospective residents through your community aims to make them feel right at home. You want them to be able to picture themselves in your residences, living in your community, and enjoying your amenities. This can be tough with an empty apartment and a "ghost town" feel.

Either approach, all demonstrations are best when a full sensory experience is offered instead of just a visual experience. However, before even broaching the task of staging, a few items need to be properly checked off the list.

Plan the Work and Work the Plan.

It can be very time-consuming and costly if staging is executed too fast and haphazardly. When planned appropriately, budgets can be met, professionals can be hired, and the project will be less overwhelming and can be completed much quicker. In addition, the plan can be replicated whenever needed for future vacant units. Keep these overall tasks in mind as you prepare your plan.

Repairs

Make a comprehensive checklist of repairs that are needed on a regular basis. Once it is completed, with each new vacancy or plan for models, you can quickly assess which repairs are needed before staging begins. Be sure to look for these often-overlooked repairs.

- From the parking lot to the bathroom, keep everything maintained.

- Sand and touch up or repaint peeling or scuffed finishes.

- Broken light fixtures and burnt bulbs.

- Shabby doors, carpets, damaged trim, or doors must be repaired or replaced.

Clean Up

Another helpful checklist would be for all cleaning tasks in the unit. Do a full examination of the apartment and take the time to clean and ensure that your apartment looks its best. Be sure the following are listed so nothing is left dirty or messy.

- Walls are clean

- Carpets are cleaned and deodorized

- Light Fixtures

- Oven

- Refrigerator

- Stovetop

- Washer/Dryer

- Microwave

- Light switches and doorknobs are sanitized

Decorating Considerations

Overall, a plan for paint colors, furniture including layout and accessories needs to be decided upon in order to get the longest gain out of the staging plan.

Colors. Neutral colors will allow the space to appeal to a wider audience. While bright colors and edgy style may really pique the interest of some, it could adversely turn off others. When staging your residence, make sure to keep the colors, styles, and materials being used as neutral and as clean as possible. They will want to imagine how they will use the space in their own style, so you want to create a residence that any prospective resident can call their own. Keeping things neutral can help make this a reality.

Style. If your community is in an upscale downtown area, keep the décor chic and modern. If you are in a "hip" area, go for something funkier and more midcentury modern. If you are in a family-friendly suburb, choose comfortable and contemporary furnishings. Adapt the furniture and accessories to the tastes of the residents in the area.

Budget. With every good plan, comes a good budget. Spend your money on repairs, maintenance, furnishings, and accessories that will create the most positive impact for your target demographic.

Paint. A fresh coat of paint on the walls will transform any room or unit instantly. It refreshes the space and keeps it looking bright and clean. If a residence is toured frequently, you may wish to paint it once a year or every other year. A pro-tip is to do away with any dark colors, and to repaint the space with light tones so you can make the rooms appear larger!

Furniture. It's a good idea to invest in staging furniture. Potential renters like to imagine what it will be like to live in a space. It's awfully hard for them to do that when a room is empty.

- Invest in some neutral-colored, classic furniture.

- If you have multiple-sized rentals, then consider investing in modular furniture that you can tailor to each space.

- Use furniture to maximize space. Open space sells, and using your furnishings and décor to open up a space is best.

- For smaller rooms, strategically place furniture to make the space appear larger.

Flooring. Choose something that goes with a lot of things and is also a bit unique. You won't want to bore your prospective residents with something they've seen at every other place they've looked at. Give them a reason to want to pick your place.

- **Main Rooms.** Give them wood floors with a distressed look. It goes with a lot of decor choices but looks fancier than your basic laminate flooring. It also holds up well to wear and tear and only needs to be refinished periodically.

- **Bathroom.** One plain color makes for a boring bathroom. Add some decorative tile in the shower and make it attractive. Bathrooms are one of the number one places that people like to see beauty when they look at their future home. Putting the extra time and effort into making it look nice will really attract people to the vibe you are sending out.

Fixtures and Appliances. Add a nice faucet to the kitchen sink. Put in a colorful backsplash. There are quite a few ways to brighten up a kitchen. Pick a color scheme where they can pull in color touches of their own and make it still look fabulous. Silver and stainless steel reflect colors and can brighten up a room.

Lamps & Light Fixtures. Potential renters love open bright spaces. Investing in a few lamps can help you brighten up any space. Make sure to get a nice variety of floor lamps, table lamps, and task lamps. Then you can strategically place them around the space to lighten dark or gloomy areas. Also, pay attention to the wattage and color spectrum of your bulbs. You want something that feels warm but is also bright enough that they can see all the great features.

Door & Cabinet Knobs. Refreshing the kitchen or bathroom can be one of the most impactful staging processes, but a remodel can cost thousands and thousands of dollars. A really simple and low-cost way to freshen up the space while keeping things inexpensive is to simply change the knobs on doors and cabinetry.

Area Rugs. Area rugs pull double duty in staging. First, they help style the home, bringing color and warmth to different areas. Secondly, area rugs will protect your flooring. You'll have a lot of foot traffic when you show a rental. If you've just replaced the floors, you'll want to keep them clean. Place area rugs in the high-traffic areas to avoid damage and add a welcome mat to the front door. Avoid any potential slip or trip hazards by securing the rug to the flooring with special tape or use a rubber mat under the rug to prevent it from sliding.

Mirrors. Mirrors aren't just for checking out your looks, they're also pretty amazing tools for interior decorating. In smaller or darker spaces, use mirrors to reflect space and light to give the appearance of a larger room. The apartment will feel open and brighter by placing mirrors opposite windows or light sources for a little investment.

Linens. Go white with bathroom linens. A clean and spacious bathroom is a must for many, and nothing makes the bathroom of a model look cleaner, and the space look larger than white linens. Add colorful, whimsical accents to make the bathroom stand out and memorable.

Décor. A little décor can go a long way, and decorating your apartment can be inexpensive and effective. Add in a few vases, picture frames, or pieces of artwork. Just give the space the personality it needs to stand out amongst all the other communities a prospect may consider.

Seasonal Accessories. Regarding accessories, seasonal items are the best way to invest your money. Home decor trends come and go. Choosing seasonal accessories will help you avoid having to buy new accessories every time tastes change. Grab some things for spring, summer, fall, and winter, and use them based on the time of year.

Furniture Covers and Storage Containers. It may be necessary to dismantle your model and store the furnishings and accent pieces. To keep your accessories and furniture looking new, you'll have to protect them. Investing in a few plastic containers and some furniture covers will protect your investments and increase the longevity of your investment in staging supplies. Plus, it will make it easier to pack and move your items.

Staging Mistakes to Avoid

When you take prospective resident on a demonstration, you're giving them their first glimpse into life within your community. Because of this, staging your model is incredibly important, and just as the right staging can turn a prospect into a resident, the wrong staging can send them running in the opposite direction. Here are some staging mistakes that you may not realize.

Personal Items. You may think that having personal items within view makes the space feel more like "home," but this actually isn't the case. When a space is too personal, it's difficult for touring prospects to take the personal out and imagine the space as their own, which could lead them to go elsewhere. Not to mention, the average tour lasts between 10 and 30 minutes. Each minute they spend scanning the space and having their attention fall on personal items is a minute that isn't focused on the space itself.

Wrong Colors. We've mentioned the importance of choosing neutral colors within your models; however, neutral doesn't have to mean boring. Layering with different neutral tones can give a pop of interest without being considered shocking, like pops of bright reds, yellows, etc. Color can also create depth, warmth, and a comforting feeling.

Room Size and Furnishings. When it comes to the residence size, you want to maximize, not minimize. Large open spaces are considerably more attractive to prospective residents. Choosing large furnishings for a small space will make it look smaller; choosing small furnishings for a large space will look awkward and cold. Like Goldilocks, you want to find the perfect middle ground. Picking the wrong furnishing options in terms of scale will give touring residents an inaccurate view of the space in each room.

Poor Lighting. A well-lit space is welcoming, friendly, and visible. Consider the lighting you have available and provide a space with lots of natural light. If there is not a lot of natural light, supplement with artificial light from a lamp, overhead light fixture, or wall sconce.

Keep the Theatrics Simple. It may be tempting to set a dining room table in a model formally, but it's best to keep things simple. Avoid becoming too theatrical with candelabras on the table, or bowls of fruit on the counter. Keep it simple and welcoming.

Your staging mistakes could be unknowingly costing you prospective residents, and now you are fully informed on how to reap great rewards with sensational staging.

Preparing Your Model or Vacant Apartment for Demonstration

Before showing the unit and demonstrating with a potential resident, be sure to take care of the following matters.

Clean Up. After a renter moves out, be sure to do a full examination of the apartment and do a thorough cleaning; ensure that your apartment looks its best after the cleaning.

Dust. Keep dust at bay by dusting the unit frequently. You never know when someone is going to show up and request to see your model unit or a vacant apartment. If they see the dust piling up, they will start to question things like air quality and the ventilation systems in your units. This may cause them to doubt how you will care for them after they move in.

Kitchens and Bathrooms. These rooms are probably the dirtiest places in any house or apartment. This is where a lot of the messy action takes place. Show off these rooms with clutter-free countertops, shiny faucets, and clean tile and grout. Make sure that visitors see that your homes are spotless and that they can have a spotless home too.

Closet Spaces. While tucked away, closets are actually a huge selling point for many prospective residents. Staging a closet is often forgotten, but it can make a huge positive impact if done correctly. A neatly staged closet with some organizational furnishings and hangers can give prospective residents a good look into what they can do in terms of effective storage ideas within the space.

Patio Space. If the unit has a patio or balcony space, don't clog it up with a bunch of junk or use it as a storage area. And don't neglect cleaning out there, either. Ensure that your visitors can view the patio as a welcome outdoor living space to the apartment's interior. If it has a view, be sure to show it off.

Minor Repairs. Even minor damage can have a big impact on the way that potential renters view an apartment. Be sure to take care of repairs as soon as you notice an issue. Keep all of your apartments in good shape.

The Little Things. Be sure to check often for the small details in the space. Have fresh towels in the bathroom and kitchen. Be sure all the light bulbs are working. Have candles strategically placed around the room. The little things will really set you apart and make your place stand out, so be sure that they stand out and are clean.

14: PHOTOGRAPHY & VIDEOGRAPHY

Essential Tools for Demonstrating Aesthetic Excellence

The first thing you'll want to do when approaching your apartment and community photography is to invest in a good camera. While you can take smartphone photos and videos and upload them online, you won't get the same photo quality in most cases. Even without editing, a camera will provide more even tones, less lens flare, and more contrast in your photos.

Add Video to Your Community Marketing

Video is a marketing trend that is sweeping industries across the board. For those in property management, a video may be that one little tidbit of the effective marketing you're missing. There is so much you can say using just a short video! Make the most of your marketing efforts, and in today's day and age, this means taking advantage of what video has to offer.

Identify the purpose of your video to make it the most impactful. A video with footage of your community, your residents enjoying their lifestyle, the inside of the residences, the amenities, and the grounds can show viewers everything they need to see to cement their decision to come in for a visit and take a genuine interest in what you have to offer. Along with this footage, some quick explanations of how to contact your community staff and some facts about your community, services, and amenities enhance the video to entice your audience better. This video doesn't need to be long. Anywhere from 30 seconds to a minute may be perfectly fine!

If a shorter video is more your style, perhaps showcase a particular apartment, amenity, or a new feature, you may want to shoot your footage and upload it to your social networks.

The videos you film can be used on your website, social media platforms, and YouTube. Viewers will use them as a great point of reference when they want to consider your community repeatedly. There is something special that an audience gains from a video that cannot be gained through written information or photographs, which is why it's become such a massive hit in community marketing!

Another excellent advantage these photo and video-sharing platforms offer is a way to cross-post to other social media sites so you can reach your entire following simultaneously. Using Instagram, for example, you can take a photo or mini-video and, with a few clicks, share it across your Instagram, Twitter, and Facebook pages all at once, allowing you to share these posts organically through multiple channels. This also allows a way for current followers on Facebook, for instance, to find your Instagram account, so you can easily branch out.

Two Dozen Top Video and Photo Shoot Tips

Because social media is a popular vehicle for marketing and advertising apartment rentals, creating the best visual first impression of your product is essential. Whether you or a paid professional are taking pictures or videos, professional-looking photos, and videos are necessary.

Preparation. There is a lot of planning and prep work for any type of photo shoot. It may seem a little much, but when you see the videos and photos, you will see how much better the outcome.

- Vacuum, dust, and clean all surfaces - including windows! You may not think that a bit of dust or a smear on a window makes a difference, but it certainly does. The camera does not overlook these details so you can't either. Use fresh flowers in every shot. You can reuse the flowers using different vases in different rooms.

- Include fresh orange juice in juice glasses in a kitchen or breakfast room shot.

- Place fresh fruit (strawberries are great) in glass bowls or on white plates along with items such as croissants, etc.

- In bedrooms, place an attractive tray somewhere using the above food/drink on the tray, along with a magazine and bright-colored cloth napkins. The tray could be set on the bed or a side table.

- We don't condone the use of candles by residents; however, in a video or photo, if you use candles, light them. Candles can also be reused in different shots in different rooms.

- In the dining room, kitchen, and living room shots use wine glasses filled with cranberry juice. It looks like the real thing but costs less. Don't forget the fresh flowers, plates with fruit, cheese, crackers, etc.

- Slightly open the blinds of windows to let light in, but not so you can see what's outside.

- Fluff any drapes but leave them open.

- Hide all cords! That means cable, electrical and window blinds.

- Keep toilet seats in closed position.

- Fluff pillows and flatten/smooth out bed linens. Don't forget to tuck in all sheets.

- Add accessories to a kitchen such as a bowl of one kind of fresh fruit. For example, all green apples or all red apples, oranges, pears, or lemons. Place a cookbook and accents to add color but not clutter.

- Place a few magazines on coffee tables.

- Add a laptop on a desk.

- In bathrooms, be sure to stage appropriately. For an "adult" bathroom, add water and bubbles to the tub along with candles and spa accessories. Don't forget the fake wine. For children's bathrooms, add toys and bubbles. Don't forget the rubber duckies and a little stool to stand on to brush teeth.

- In kitchens and bathrooms, tuck the sides of any towels in and make sure no tags are showing.

- Temporarily remove all area rugs or bathroom rugs. Rooms will appear bigger and more spacious in photos or videos without rugs.

Take Enough Photos. You don't want to take and post hundreds of pictures, because no one wants to take the time look through all of those. Instead make sure that you take and post enough pictures of your community that potential residents see all your great features. Typically, you want to have around 10-15 photos that include the model and or available apartment, interior and exterior amenities, common areas and community features.

Focus on Features. Take a minute to look at your competition's listings and figure out your competitive advantage, in other words, what makes your community so special that it stands out against your competition. Then, when you take pictures of your property focus on your most unique and exciting features.

Lighting. Prospects want to see plenty of light and bright and airy space, so you'll need to play with what you have to convey the benefit of the lighting in your apartments and community amenity spaces. With artificial light, using layered light really creates an even and bright appeal. Most cameras will adjust to the brightest light in the room, so stand back out of the light source and focus the camera away from where the light is coming from for maximum impact.

- Take photos during a time of day when the sunlight is most likely to shine through. Take the screens off windows to increase the light from outside. Ask maintenance to remove the screens before you take your photos and to put them back on at the completion of the photo shoot.

- Turn all lights on, and if necessary, add spotlights hidden by furniture to make a room even brighter.

- Make sure there are no reflections from any lights from the glass on pictures, mirrors, and windows. Changing the angle of the shot can eliminate the reflection.

Location. Location. Location. The location also matters, and where you take your photos will really impact how your photos turn out.

- When taking a photo of an interior apartment and community amenity or any interior space, try standing in the corner and taking the photo in a broad landscape fashion. Shooting a photo head-on will tend to make the room look smaller and more claustrophobic, while the corner technique will give a great impression of the size of the space. You want to take a photo from an angle that makes the spaces look large and open.

- One of the best things about digital cameras or smartphone use is that you can take hundreds of pictures. So, when taking photos, experiment a bit with different angles. Try photos from different eye levels and from different areas of the room. Then when you go through your pictures, you can pick out the best ones and begin using them right away.

- Do not be afraid to edit. You don't want to saturate your pictures with filters so they end up looking completely doctored, but you can tweak them a little to highlight the features. Play with brightness, color, and even cropping to make sure that you are presenting the best possible photo of the space, just be careful not to overdo it.

Classic Listing Photo Mistakes to Avoid

Your listing photography is the first introduction to your potential renters. The very first thing anyone does before even reading the details of the space is look at the photos. If the photos aren't good, they'll quickly move on to the next listing without even giving your rental a chance. It is essential that you offer up great listing photography to engage potential renters and entice them to learn more. There are some pretty common mistakes property managers make when creating listing photography.

Blurry or Small Photos. Blurry and small photos can be a huge problem, because if the picture isn't clear, then no one can see the great amenities of your property. So before listing any photos, do a little editing to ensure that anyone can look quickly at a photo and see all the important things you want to highlight. If the photo is bad quality, scrap it and take a new one. Also, make sure once you have a great set of photos that you load them onto the listing site with the full file size. If you take great photos and end up listing them with small file size, you'll lose the picture quality you worked so hard to obtain.

Cluttered Backgrounds. We've all seen the listing photos where there's piles of laundry in the corner or stacks of moving boxes. This kind of picture will not attract any potential renters, so make sure to time your listing photography where you have sharp and clean backgrounds and can really highlight the space.

Over Editing. On the other end of the spectrum are property managers who use too many soft filters, turn the contrast up too high, and use too much warmth so that the property ends up looking like a cartoon. It's not a bad idea to make some adjustments to your photos to lighten the space or focus on a great amenity, but you can also get too heavy-handed. If your photos are too edited, it will look like you are trying to cover up something, which will definitely turn off potential renters.

Upload Issues. Finally, even if you have taken the best photos in the world but upload them incorrectly, you can have all kinds of issues, from upside-down photos to pixilation from low-quality files to photos that don't fit in the provided photo frames. Make sure that once you've uploaded your listing, you scroll through to make sure you've done it all correctly and it that the listing along with the photos look good so you don't turn off potential occupants.

Tips for Great Listing Photography

With so many people looking online for their next home, you must ensure you stand out from your competition. One of the best ways to garner interest and attract potential residents is with great listing photography. Focus on the systems that will reach your audience, and everyone will notice your fabulous marketing and social media efforts.

INDEX

MEET ELAINE SIMPSON

Elaine Simpson is a passionate businesswoman, international speaker, consultant, author, and trainer specializing in everything multi-family. With over 35 years of experiencing the industry's good, bad, and ugly, Elaine is recognized as the Property Management Expert. Using her knowledge, experience, and innovative ideas, Elaine Simpson implements customized solutions for property management professionals worldwide, resulting in increased income and reduced vacancies.

 Ms. Simpson is the creator of The Property Management Adult Coloring Book, author of The Indispensable Handbook for Property Managers and Close The Back Door, and founder and editor of the magazine Occupancy Solutions, the only magazine dedicated to the onsite property management professional. Ms. Simpson is a licensed real estate broker in Michigan and Arizona, a Certified Senior Real Estate Specialist, an Accredited Resident Manager, an NAA EI Faculty member, and a Certified Assisted Housing Manager.

Connect with Elaine!

Web: www.OccupancySolutions.com

Twitter: @occupancysolved

Facebook: facebook.com/OccupancySolutions

Instagram: @elainem.simpson and @occupancysolutionsllc

LinkedIn: linkedin.com/in/elaine-esimpson/ and linkedin.com/company/occupancy-solutions-LLC/

About Occupancy Solutions

We Put a Brighter Spotlight on Your Property!

We provide a complete assessment of your business. We look at what is and is not working, evaluate current systems, and find solutions. This process can be as detailed as you want. After we review your business

OCCUPANCY
SOLUTIONS, LLC

assessment with you, we devise a plan of action specifically tailored to your company. Then we implement the system with one-on-one training and coaching with your team to help you achieve your goals.

We Can Help Ensure the Proper Execution of Your Property Management Plan

Creating a plan is the easy part; implementation is key to the success of any plan. Now comes the challenge - ensuring your team not only understands the plan but that your team knows how to deliver consistent execution of the plan so you can meet your goals. This can be frustrating and overwhelming, especially since this plan is in addition to everything else you and your team are trying to do. Let Occupancy Solutions help you implement your plan with daily oversight, team-building focus, and ongoing support and coaching of your team so you can move forward and achieve success.

Why? Because while focusing on things like marketing and leasing agreements is important, your employees and how you train and develop them will have just as much of an impact on your bottom line. With our plan implementation coaching, we can help you every step of the way.

Occupancy Solutions is dedicated to helping you, your team, and your community improve to increase income. With our range of solutions, services, and training, we can help you reach your full potential. For more information about our services, call us at (800) 865-0948 today.